"The HAPI Book"

High Achiever Piano Instructor

Roger C. Hayden

authorHOUSE®

AuthorHouse™
1663 Liberty Drive
Bloomington, IN 47403
www.authorhouse.com
Phone: 1 (800) 839-8640

Published by AuthorHouse   05/05/2015

ISBN: 978-1-4969-7429-7 (sc)
ISBN: 978-1-4969-7430-3 (e)

Print information available on the last page.

Acknowledgements

I am eternally grateful to God, for His providence, gifts and opportunities. I am joyfully grateful to the parents of students whose love, encouragement, prayers and diligence at home helped these methods to bear fruit and rapidly grow amazing young musicians. I remain pleased and delighted with our students from seven to seventy five having learned from the HAPI Book, proving what can be accomplished. And thanks to our friend and artist, Tracy Burner for her lively, playful illustrations that convey the HAPI Book's 'can do' confidence. And to my amazing wife, Jane, the best and loveliest any man ever had, for her help, encouragement, patience and inspiration.

"Play to Learn" swiftly and joyfully *or 'Learn to Play', painfully, tediously!*

What makes the HAPI Book happy is that students play a lot more piano in lot less time. Life is short. Learning to play the piano does not need to be agonizing and slow.

A shortcut is different path to get you someplace faster. It may not be easier, it may also be an adventure, but *faster with fascination* might be best. These shortcuts do not leave the pianist ill equipped, on the contrary, foundations are everything, and the mix of skills used here can inspire reading, playing by ear, improvisation, and brilliant dexterity. You will come to know 'the keys'.

These methods work because from the first they employ the eye, ear and hand, the three most powerful stimulators for learning and retaining. These high volume motivations are reinforced with pleasurable and profitable repetition. It's no wonder they learn FAST!! *(Intelligence growth in children who learn music for six months has been measured to grow as much as ten percent. Neuroscientists report that a strong percentage of the brain is set aside for small muscle control, especially the hand. Music links the hand with the eye and the ear, development is rapid, natural and expected.)*

Considered separately, here are several elements, and why they work.

1. **Finger Patterns, Hold Patterns and Reach Patterns (Hand Training, based on European 19th Century Traditions)**

THESE ARE VERY IMPORTANT because these patterns simultaneously grow many skills.

Melodic Dexterity:
Individual finger strength and control
> Fingers in many combinations
> Accurate Key finding, familiarity with the keyboard
> Hands are ready to play complex passages LONG before they can be read!

Rhythmic Development: the beat, meters and phrasing are quickly linked to the hand and heart.
Finger patterns practiced with a strong even beat and grow natural musicianship.
> Familiarity with the keyboard is quick and enjoyable.
> Strong Rhythm is a **FAST TEACHER**!

Ear Training
> Patterns train the ear. Wrong notes and wrong rhythms instinctively demand correction.
> Fingers begin to automatically reach for sharps and flats

Harmonic Discernment
> These patterns contribute to rapid harmonic comprehension and control. Harmony delights us. The HAPI Book is rich with engaging interesting harmony.

2. **2. Music Looks Like it Sounds (Eye, Ear and Logic)**

> Music notation is visually logical; it LOOKS like it SOUNDS. Utilizing patterns in interesting pieces, the eye begins to intuitively gather visual information needed to read music. No advanced pianist reads individual lines and spaces, any more than a reader sees every letter. (Although note names must be learned.) Musicians read patterns. The HAPI Book takes advantage of patterning; and the music we love is made of delightful patterns.

3. **Demonstrate And Imitate Songs (Touch and Pitch Training, hand and ear)**

   Unique, fun pieces (especially Black Key Songs) learned by rote and watching. The teacher must play them skillfully and musically, then guide the student allowing simple imitation. (The Haydenpiano.com Website also demonstrates these pieces.) Early joy is achieved by sending them home with music to play. Early reading is done by frequently pointing out the logic, on the written page, of music notation. **Do not fear that they may play it by ear, instead welcome and utilize this common gift!**

4. **Rhythm Reading in only Two Stages**

   Stage one: accomplishes the **rhythmic names** of notes and **musical timing**. By **Speaking them Rhythmically** the tongue becomes a natural metronome. Rhythm is seen, felt and internalized.
   Stage two: Start counting beats when 16th notes are utilized. Numbering the beats with syllable subdivisions becomes easy once the big values are felt using Stage one. (See Haydenpiano.com Website demo.)

   Visually obvious Eighth and Quarter notes are employed from the beginning because their appearance makes the 'twice as fast' relationship easy to see and perform. Dexterity comes quickly with finger patterns; eighth notes visually help the fingers move.

5. **Transposing into all keys**

   Dexterity from the finger patterns and diatonic scale repetitions equip students audibly to reach for the correct keys instinctively. For many players the sight and sound of the intervals become automatic, which is how advanced players read rapidly.

   Students should often watch music notation, even if memorized; so that the visual associations combined with hearing and touch strengthen reading. Hands led by sound and a practiced touch free the eyes to discern and read.

6. **Black Key Songs**

   The black keys are pentatonic and easy to find, and many musical delights can result from their utilization. A major benefit is the common fear of multiple sharp and flat keys is lessened.

7. **High Expectations**

   Expecting students to be thinking, reaching, and achieving, the HAPI Book assumes intelligence, and a childlike desire to learn. Give them the joy of exploration and problem solving.

8. **Balance between Difficult and Easy.**

   Some pieces are hard, a bit complex, and slow to achieve, but then, growth is faster. Easy reading pieces often follow, allowing students a sense of forward motion. Rapid growth is felt and enjoyed.

9. **Interesting Harmony and Rhythms**

   The HAPI Book does not shy from unusual yet interesting harmonies, melodies and rhythms.

10. **Four Simple Songs about Lines and Spaces, plus other unique theory application pages.**

    Learning lines and spaces and their assigned keys should not take long. Assume and drill key finding as the songs increase in range.

11. **Smaller Print forces discernment of detail, accelerates 'seeing', (note font sizes in our electronic devices)**

    The HAPI Book asks students to see the small steps and skips. They CAN see! Teach them to LOOK and play. **Music Notation is Logical! Expect intelligence, teach a principle, ask the question, and be silent until they give the answer. Make their 'wheels turn'.**

12. **For written theory we enjoy the "Alfred's Essentials of Music Theory" Teacher's Activity Kit, Book 1, 2 & 3**

    30 Reproducible Activities, Plus 6 Tests. A page per week is reproduced and given to each student. Or buy the book and do it for yourself. ISBN-13: 978-07390-0873-7

    For more help, demonstrations and explanations go to: www.haydenpiano.com.

    Poems provided above many songs are all original and copyrighted creations by Roger C Hayden.
    Yours, with prayer and confidence,   Roger C Hayden

All contained Finger, Hold and Reach Patterns and the pages where found

p. 3	FP 1,2	HP (1) 5 5 5	RP (1-5) 3 3 3
p. 6	FP 2 3	HP (1) 4 4 4	RP (1-5) 2 2 2
p. 9	F P 3, 4	H P (1) 2 2 2	R P (1-5) 4 4 4
p. 13	F P 4, 5	H P (1) 3 3 3	R P (1-5) 2 2 3
p. 16	F P 1,2,3	H P (1) 3 4 5	R P (1-5) 4 4 3
p. 21	FP 2,3,4,	H P (1) 3 4 3	R P (1-5) 4 2 3
p. 24	F P 3,4,5,	H P (5) 1 1 1	R P (1-5) 2 3 4 2 3
p. 27	F P 1,2,3,4	H P (5) 3 1 2 1 2	R P (1-5) 4 2 4 2 3
p. 30	F P 2,3,4,5	H P (5) 3 1 3 2 1	R P (1-5) 3 3 4 2 3
p. 33	F P 1 2 3 4 5 r	H P (5) 4 4 3 2 1	R P (1 sixth 5) 4 3 2 3 3
p. 35	F P 1 2 3 4 3 4	H P (4) 1 2 3 2 1 2 1	R P (1 sixth 5) 2 3 2 3 2 3 2
p. 36	F P 3 4 5 3 2 1	H P (4) 1 2 1 3 1	R P (1 sixth 5) 4 2 3 2 3
p. 44	F P 2 3 4 5 1 5	H P (3) 5 1 5	R P (1 sixth 5) 4 3 4 3 2
p. 48	F P 2 3 2 3 4 5 4 5	H P (4) 3 2 1	R P (1 sixth 5) 2 3 4 2 4
p. 51	F P 3 4 3 4 2 3 2 3	H P (3) 4 4 5	R P (1 sixth 5) 4 2 2 3 3
p. 54	F P 3 4 5 2 3 4 3 2 1	H P (5) 4 2 3 1 2 2 1	R P 1 2 1 3 1 4 1 5
p. 57	F P 1 4 3 2	H P 3 (4) 1 2 1 2 1 2	R P (1-3) 2 2 2 4 5 4 5
p. 61	F P 1 2 3 4 5 4 3 4	H P (4) 3 2 1 1 1 3 5	R P 1 2 1 3 1 4 1 5 1 5 1 5 C D C E C F C G C A C B
p. 65	F P 3 4 5 1 3 5 4 3 1	H P 3 4 (5) 1 2 1 2 1	R P (1 sixth 5) 4 3 2 3 2 3 2
p. 68	FP 5 4 5 3 4 2 3 1	H P (5) 3 4 2 3 1 2 1	RP (1) 5 4 5 2 4 2 3
p. 73	F P 1 2 3 4 3 4 3 5 4	H P (5) 4 2 3 (1) 2 3 4	RP (1) (sixth) 5 3 4 2 3
p. 75	F P 5 3 4 2 3 1	H P (3) 4 2 5 1 5 1 5	R P (5) (sixth) 1 4 2 3 2 3 1
p. 81	F P 1 5 2 5 3 5	H P (5) 4 1 4 2 4 1 4	R P (1 seventh 5) 2 3 2
p. 87	F P 4 3 2 5 4 3 2 1	H P 1 4 3 (2) 5 4 5 4	R P 1 octave (5) 4 3 2 3 2 3
p. 91	F P 1 5 2 4 2 3	H P (3) 1 5 1 4 2 5 1	R P 1 octave (5) 4 3 2 2 3 2
p. 93	F P 3 4 3 2 1 2 3 1	H P (4) 3 1 2 1 2	R P (1-5) 3 3 2 2 4 4 3
p. 95	F P 2 4 5 4 3 4 3 4	H P (1) 3 4 3 5 4 3 2	R P (1-5) 4 3 4 3 2 4 3

High Achiever Piano Instructor   R C Hayden   ix

Weekly Method for Performing Patterns

Originator
Anne Vanko Liva

One each of a Finger pattern, Hold pattern and Reach pattern is assigned weekly. The Patterns in music notation are performed as you see below. A steady, even beat is essential, with clean, even tones. These are CRUCIAL to your success.

Compiled & Arr. R C Hayden

The Left Hand will mirror the pattern as follows, moving down an octave.

Right Hand hold pattern,

Left Hand Hold Pattern

Reach Pattern, Right Hand

Reach Pattern, Left Hand descending

These sequences are not sacred. Make up more of your own. Have students make them up, (student's creations are often harder). You may want to move on to scales, Hanon, or other of technic studies. Insist on a rhythmic, energetic, performance, always listening for evenness of touch. For variety alternate ƒ with p. When they become easy, suggest higher tempos as long as a precise even touch is kept. Insist on their listening to every stroke; students like the challenge and enjoy the feeling of controlled rhythmic speed.

Contents

The Two Finger Black Key Song

Lyrics, RC Hayden

Rote Learned: Demonstrate, Imitate
Play and teach by Ear, Eye and Imitation
Send the new student home with a SONG!

Folk

Right Hand third finger plays notes with stems up.

Left Hand third finger plays ONLY F#'s (stems down)

If I have a cou - ple fin - gers I can play and help the sing - ers,

The Right Hand will cross over the left

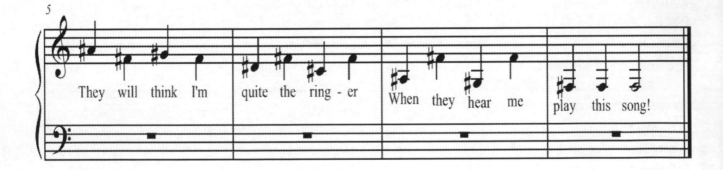

They will think I'm quite the ring - er When they hear me play this song!

Music Looks like it Sounds ! !

Music Notation is simple when compared to a written language of totally symbolic letters and words,

It is made of visual patterns that can be seen,

Wag the Thumb

Lots of Lift to the thumb. then Seesaw with lots of lift on 1 and 2, Lift and Slap.   **R C Hayden**

Use the note's Rhythm Names to learn their rhythmic relationship.

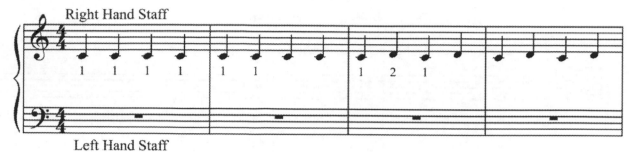

Rhythm Note Names

At First, Clap and say the Rhythm Note Names

Then Play and Sing the Rhythm Note Names on the indicated Piano keys.

Then Play and Sing the Key Names using correct rhythm

Lastly, Play and Sing the Finger Numbers using correct rhythm

R C Hayden

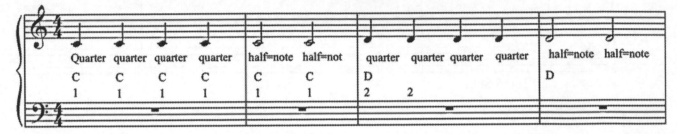

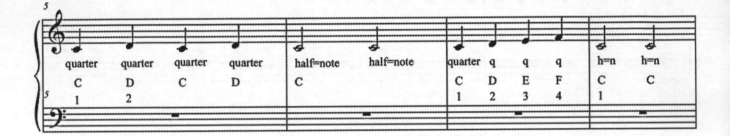

Little Bitty Mouse

First Week: Hands Separately: Fingerings: 1,2,1,2,1 Later HT if possible.
Second Week   1,3,1,3,1 Third Week 1,4,1,4,1. Later 1,2,3,4,5

R C Hayden

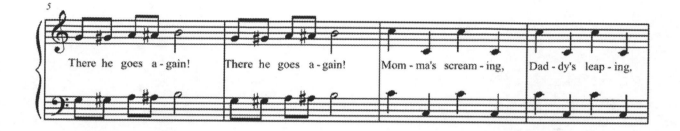

The Juggler
Right Hand Left Hand

R C Hayden

©May 28, 2014

FP 2 3   HP (1) 4 4 4   RP (1-5) 2 2 2

Find all the A B C's

Start to know the Letter Names of the keys.

  There are only seven, A B C D E F G.

    Memorize where A is, (upper white key inside the three black key group).

  And memorize where C is.

    Then find and memorize Middle C.

R C Hayden

The Piano's lowest key is an A

    Play all the A's.   Play all the C's.   Find Middle C.

    How many A's are on an acoustic piano (and full size keyboards)? _____

    How many keys are there from one A to the next A, (counting whites and blacks)? _____

    What is an Interval? _____

    How is an Interval 'Named"? _____

    Begin NOW to teach your eye to see INTERVALS, and your fingers to REACH them.

    Play and Sing the Interval Song.

The Tortoise and the Hare
The Turtle and the Rabbit

R C Hayden

The Interval Song

Play and Sing : Sing the Words
                    Sing the Rhythm Note Names
                    Sing the Key Note names
                    Sing the Finger Numbers

R C Hayden

F P 3, 4   H P (1) 2 2 2   R P (1-5) 4 4 4

Amazing Grace

This is a Pentatonic Song, using a five note scale. Using the Black Keys only place Right Thumb on F# above Middle C. Begin playing on the Left Second Finger on Middle C#, having the Left Thumb ready on D#.

John Newton

Vs 4. The Lord has promised good to me, His Word my hope secures,
He will my shield and portion be as long as life endures.

Vs 5. When we've been there ten thousand years, bright shining as the sun,
We've no less days to sing God's praise than when we'd first begun.

Merrily We Roll Along

Folk Song

Key of C

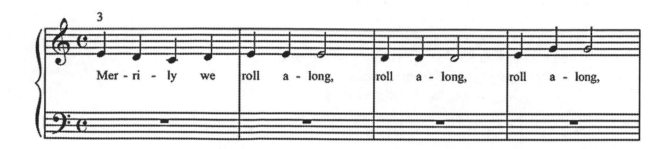

Mer - ri - ly we roll a - long, roll a - long, roll a - long,

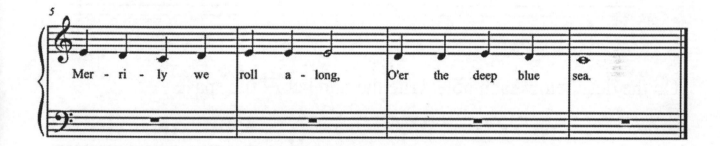

Mer - ri - ly we roll a - long, O'er the deep blue sea.

Key of F   Transpose this song, starting on A below Middle C

Key of G, Changing note values.   Transpose, starting on B below Middle C
Notice that Rhythm notation has changed,
but Rhythm relationships have not.

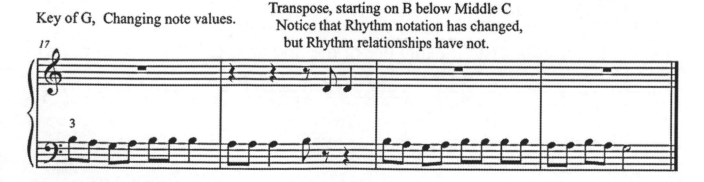

"Merrily" can also be played on Black Keys beginning on A#.

Numbering Lines and Spaces

Note finding's easy, you just have to think.
Sayings will help till it's quick as a wink..
Music can look like it Sounds, not like words,
Open Eyes, Open Ears, soon the notes can be heard.

We do it by sight and we do it by sound
And we feel with our fingers as they fly up and down
It's fun to make music, it's joy to create
Now stop, look and listen, and melody make.

We count lines and spaces from the bottom up.
On the dots below each note write the number of the line.

On the dots below each note write the number of the space.

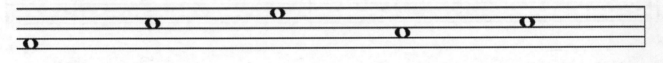

On the dots below each note write L if its a line and S if its a space.

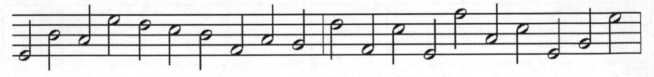

On the upper dots write L for line notes and S for space notes.
On the lower dots write the number of the line or space (from bottom up)

Note Dance

R C Hayden

Note Reading: Steps and Starter notes

FP 4, 5   H P (1) 3 5 3   R P (1-5) 2 2 3

The Fox and the Crow

R C Hayden

What wonderful feathers,
  How they shine in the light!
To see you up close
  Would be such a delight!

So Flattered and Proud
  To the ground the Crow flew,
But instead of parading
  He became a crow stew.

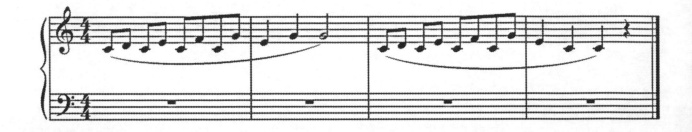

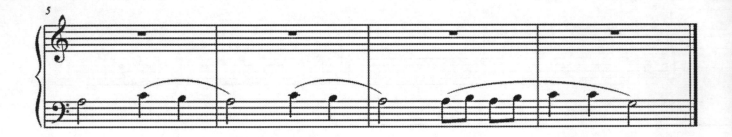

Susanna Up and Down the Steps

R C Hayden

Chasing kittens through the house
Making like a monster mouse!
When I catch my furry pet
I'll scratch her neck and stroke her back.

FP 1 2 3   H P (1) 3 4 5   R P (1-5) 4 4 3

The Wind and the Sun

R C Hayden

Grand Staff Lines and Spaces
How to know Letter Names of Lines and Spaces

Treble Clef has Five Lines, Named from the lowest to the highest E G B D G
We use the sentence Every Good Boy Does Fine to help remember their letter names.
Each Line BELONGS to a KEY on the Piano. Get to know their NAMES AND KEYS.

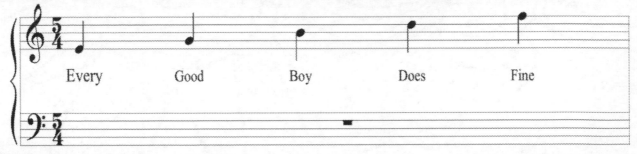

Every   Good   Boy   Does   Fine

Between the Lines are Four Spaces, and they each belong to KEYS on the piano. The spaces spell
F A C E. We like to call the Treble Clef the PEOPLE cleff.

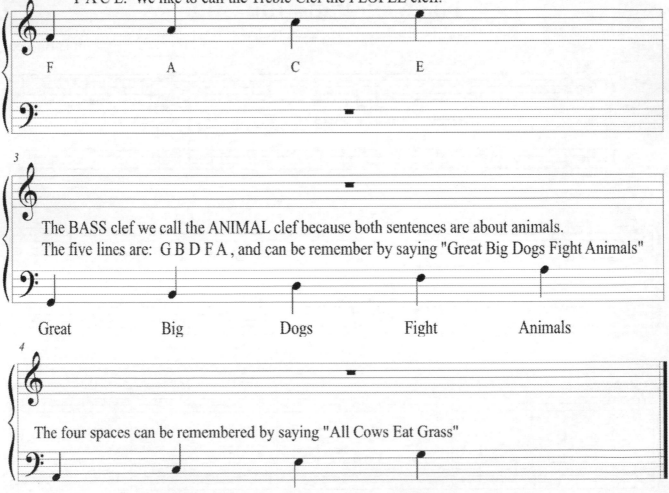

F   A   C   E

The BASS clef we call the ANIMAL clef because both sentences are about animals.
The five lines are: G B D F A , and can be remember by saying "Great Big Dogs Fight Animals"

Great   Big   Dogs   Fight   Animals

The four spaces can be remembered by saying "All Cows Eat Grass"

All   Cows   Eat   Grass

Songs by Rote and Note

This Old Man

C position starter songs

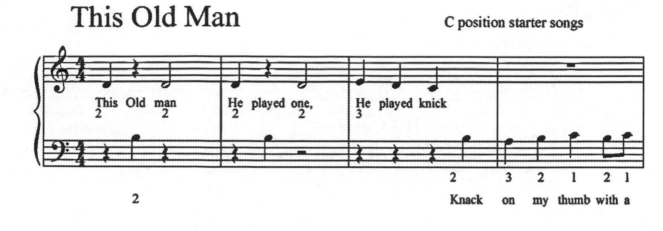

Twinkle, Twinkle Little Star

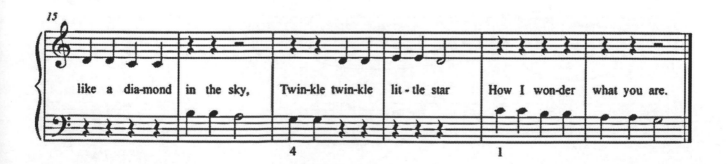

Find the C's
Use the C's
Read Patterns
Moving Hands

From C to Shining C

R C Hayden

Spider, spider on my wall
Did you take a nasty fall
One leg bent it seems to me
Your web let go, you broke a knee

The Limping Spider

R C Hayden

Reach Pattern Song

FP 2,3,4,   H P (1) 3 4 3   R P (1-5) 4 3 2

The Boy Who Cried Wolf

A Story in Song

Sheperd boy yelled "Wolf" for fun,
Just to watch his friends all run.
Then came wolf, and "Wolf" he yelled,
None beleived and none would come.

R C Hayden

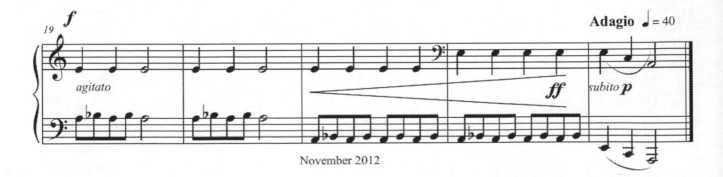

November 2012

Ode To Joy

Beethoven

Echo Valley

HELLO?   hello?
 WHO'S THERE?   who's there?
  ANYBODY?   anybody?
   ANYWHERE?   anywhere?

R C Hayden

F P 3,4,5,   H P (5) 1 1 1   R P (1-5) 2 3 4 2 3

Note Naming and Key Finding

Good Readers will Play for a lifetime.
Weak readers are done when the lessons stop !

Do a line a day, write the letter name under each note,
then find and play it on the piano.

Barn Dance

R C Hayden

Rhythm Reading, Page 2

R C Hayden

Not for playing, but for saying and clapping, one staff at a time.

Use Rhythmic note names to learn both their names and how they fit together.

16th notes require shifting to numbered beats, the best way to count.

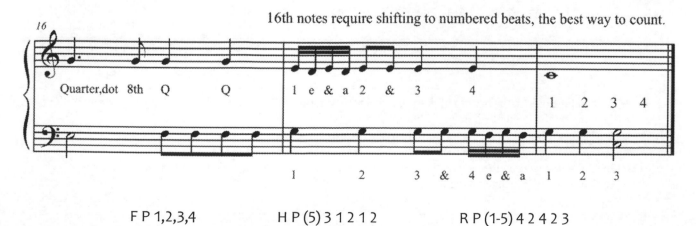

F P 1,2,3,4   H P (5) 3 1 2 1 2   R P (1-5) 4 2 4 2 3

London Bridge

Folk Songs
arr.   R C Hayden

Two fun Rote Songs to Play and to Sing

Lon   don Bridge - is   fall ing - down   fall ing - down   fall ing down -

Lon   don Bridge   is   fall - ing down, - my   fair   la dy.

There's A Hole in the Bottom of the Sea

Hole in th bot-tom of the Sea   There's a

There's a Hole in the bot-tom of the Sea   There's a

hole, there's a hole, there's a hole, there's a hole, there's a hole   in the

Bot-tom of the   Sea.

V. 2 There's a log in the hole in the bottom of the Sea . (repeat). (Chorus) There's a hole .(5 times).in the bottom of the Sea!
V. 3 There's a bump on the log in the hole in the bottom of the sea!
V.4   There's a frog on the bump on the log in the hole in the bottom of the sea!
V.5   There's a wart on the frog on the bump on the log in the hole in the bottom of the sea!
V. 6 There's a hair on the wart on the frog on the bump on the log in the hole in the bottom of the sea!
V. 7 There's a flea . . .   V. 8 There's a germ . .

Piano Key Note Finder

R C Hayden

You might think there are 88 keys on a piano, OK, Right.
But there are only Seven keys repeated over and over,
and some black keys that take their names from the whites!

Five Lines there are on every staff
To know them well can make you laugh
Tis joy to know the notes and keys
Make reading easy as a breeze.

Treble Clef Lines
Every Good Boy Does Fine

R C Hayden

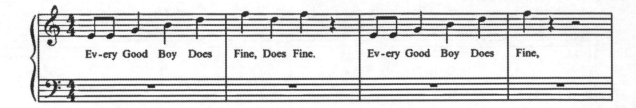

Ev-ery Good Boy Does | Fine, Does Fine. | Ev-ery Good Boy Does | Fine,

Every Good Boy Good | Boy Does Fine | Every Good Every Good | Boy Good Boy Does | Fine Does Fine Does | Fine.

Find the Keys, Spot the Intervals, Read the Patterns,

Music Sight Reading is an Eye, Ear, and Touch Game you can win quickly

Treble Clef Line Notes

You don't have time to Name every key as you play, You Do have time to spot and play patterns

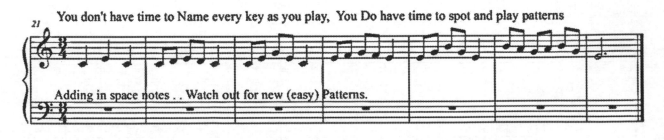

Adding in space notes . . Watch out for new (easy) Patterns.

F P 2, 3, 4, 5   H P (5) 3 1 3 2 1   R P (1-5) 3 3 4 2 3

Bass Clef Space Song

Learning Lines and Spaces of the Grand Staff
and the Exact Keys that belong to them. . . . .
Here is Song # 2 using an acrostic to help you find
and play the Bass Cleff Space keys.

The other songs are pages 28, 33 and 39
Or see page 17 for a complete list of
all the Grand Staff lines and spaces.

R C Hayden

Fairmount Park

This triplet rhythm piano song will help you learn scale fingerings in a fast entertaining way.
Be sure to bring the thumb under (measures 1 and 7) to effortlessly 'drill' the hard part of scales.
When confident, transpose to keys of G, D, A and E, finding the sharps by ear, teaching the
hands to know the keys automatically.

R C Hayden

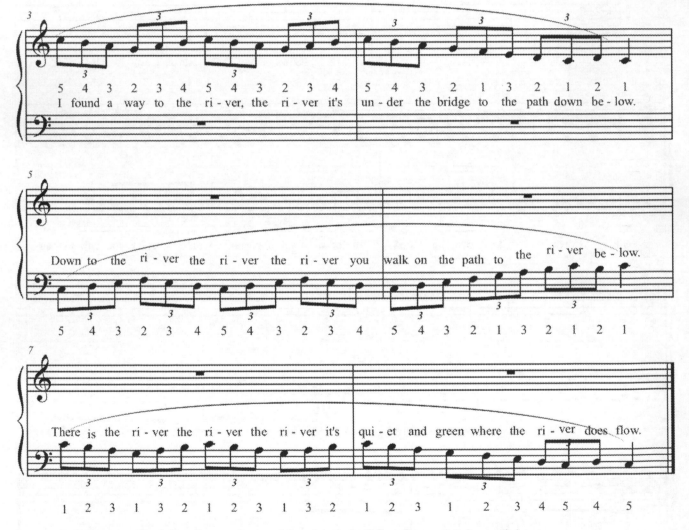

Play with a lovely, connected legato touch.

Fairmount Park is a famous very old and wonderful park running 'secretly'
through the heart of Philadelphia. It lies far below the noise and hurry, all
trees and green, sculptures, trails, lawns, water and more.

Stepping Skipping Tripping Flipping

R C Hayden

F P 1 2 3 4 5 r   H P (5) 4 4 3 2 1   R P (1 sixth 5) 4 3 2 3 3

The F A C E Song
Treble Clef Spaces

Lock into your mind's eye spaces that belong to certain keys,
It's always the same! !

R C Hayden

Car Crash

The Ugliest Song in the Book ! !

R C Hayden

Note Reader

Inner Space notes

Tag, You're It !

R C Hayden

F P 1 2 3 4 3 4   H P (4) 1 2 3 2 1 2 1 R P   (1 sixth 5) 2 3 2 3 2 3 2

It's windy, time to hit the waves
A breeze to fill the sail!
Water whispering on the hull,
Please don't hit that whale!

Gone Sailing

R C Hayden

Allegro

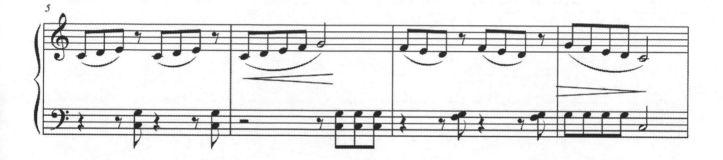

The Camel's Hump

Lazy Camel wouldn't work
Hrumph he said, Hrumph he got

For Interval Reading and Rhythm and
two hand coordination

R C Hayden

Dromedarily

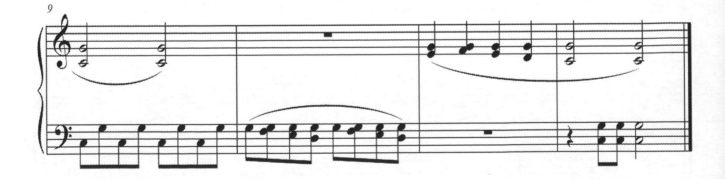

Great Big Dogs Fight Animals
Bass Clef Lines Song

R C Hayden

(Woof Woof)

Great Big Dogs,   Great Big Dogs,   Great Dogs Great Big Dogs Dogs Fight An-i-mals!

Great Big Dogs,   Great Big Dogs,   Great Big Dogs Fight An-i-mals!   -

Great Big Dogs Fight An-i-mals!   -   Poor   Poor   An-i-mals!

F P 3 4 5 3 2 1   H P (4) 1 2 1 3 1   R P (1 sixth 5) 4 3 2 3 3

Music LOOKS Like it SOUNDS

Quarter, Two Eights Half Note Rhythm

Following Notes on the Staff

R C Hayden

We use Note Letter Names to know where to begin. Then, as much as possible, see and read patterns.
   And SEE INTERVALS, See the Direction of the note patterns.
Notice when notes are on lines, and on spaces, learn how far to reach.

   MUSIC LOOKS LIKE IT SOUNDS ! !

We do not have TIME to read every note's letter name, we don't read words that way, either. We see
   PATTERNS of notes, our fingers will come to know these patterns by matching finger patterns with
   note patterns.

And learn to associate lines and spaces with KEYS on the piano, not just letter names.

Quiet morning, quieter still
Snow piling up on the window sill
Cars creep by on tippy toe tires
How loud is snow though it fell for miles!

Snowy Morning

Demonstrate/Imitate

R C Hayden

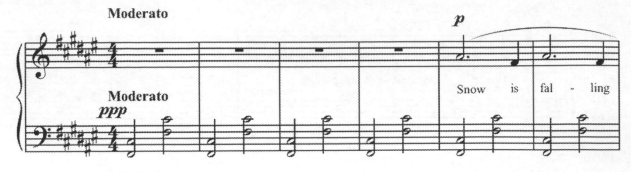

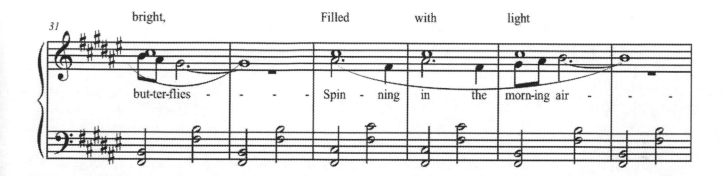

All My Ducks in a Row

R C Hayden

F P 2 3 4 5 1 5   H P (3) 5 1 5   R P (1 sixth 5) 4 3 4 3 2

Leap Frog

R C Hayden

Game Two

Game Three

Final Score

Flying down a snowy hill
Wind whipping, runners hissing
Icy bumps that jar your teeth
There's no better Winter thrill

Sleigh Ride

R C Hayden

Horse and Buggy Ride
Seeing and Reading Chords Patterns

R C Hayden

Transposing Song

First Week: Learn hands alone, then combine hands.
  Memorize, assigning your five fingers to the five consecutive keys

Second Week: Move your hand position up to D finding the needed sharp by ear to make it sound right.
  When you can play it easily, move up to E, and eventually to the rest of the white keys.

Third Week: Start on the Black Keys.

R C Hayden

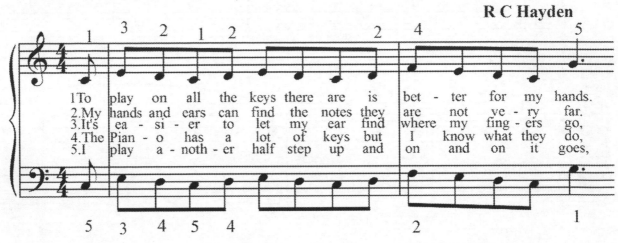

Getting to know the keys
What they do
Where they are
How they work together !

F P 2 3 2 3 4 5 4 5   H P (4) 3 2 1   R P (1 sixth 5) 2 3 4 2 4

Ode To Joy

With Simple Harmony

With Tucker Burner's Help

Beethoven

Arr. R C Hayden

Bull Frog
Black Key Song

For Alizabeth

R C Hayden

Stems up, Right Hand,   Stems down, Left Hand

Sweet Clarisse

Both Hands reading and playing in the Treble Clef. In this song stems up are for Right Hand, Stems down are for the Left Hand.

R C Hayden

Get a kiss from Sweet risse, She's so sweet you can - not miss

On the cheek she'll plant a kiss, Get a kiss from Sweet Cla - risse.

Stems Down, Left hand, Stems up, Right Hand

F P 3 4 3 4 2 3 2 3 1 2 1 2   H P (3) 4 4 5   R P (1 sixth 5) 4 2 2 3 3

The Centipede

R C Hayden

The Centipede can tred on eggs
Gently with one hundred legs.
Slow he moves but sure he goes
On all five hundred of his toes.

Apple Pie

R C Hayden

Hungrily

F P 3 4 5 2 3 4 3 2 1   H P (5) 4 2 3 1 2 2 1   R P 1 2 1 3 1 4 1 5

Transposing Song with Harmony

R C Hayden

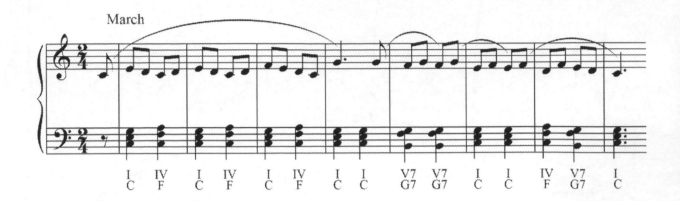

The Rocking Horse

R C Hayden

Right/Left Coordination

F P 1 4 3 2   H P 3 (4) 1 2 1 2 1 2   R P   (1-3) 2 2 2 4 5 4 5

Sunny Day

R C Hayden

Warmly

Copyright November 2012

F P 1 4 3 4 2 3 1 2   H P 3 (4) 1 2 1 2 1 2   R P (1-3) 2 2 2 4 5 4 5

Jackrabbit

Race of the Intervals

R C Hayden

Agitato

It Shines, it warms
It bakes, it burns
Brings life, and growth
With night, takes turns

Summer Sun

Demonstrate/Imitate

R C Hayden

Summer Sun

F P 1 2 3 4 5 4 3 4   H P \ (4) 3 2 1 2 3 5 1   R P 1 2 1 3 1 4 1 5 1 5 1 5
                                                             C D C E C F C G C A C B

First Sonatina

R C Hayden

Quiet Sea in C

Pedal Etude

R C Hayden

With quiet dignity

Since the harmony changes on nearly every beat, the sustain pedal must be lifted and depressed quickly and in perfect time. Lift too soon and you have staccato. Lift too late and the changing harmonies overlap and create unpleasant dissonance.

This will take practice and perseverance, and the chords in the right hand are not easy.

But it is lovely and worth the effort.

After while the ear will hear and the foot will know when to move,
then a lot of sustain pedaling will begin to become instinctive.

Galloping Geckos

R C Hayden

Note Reading
Pattern Reading

Allegretto

F P 3 4 5 1 3 5 4 3 1   H P 3 4 (5) 1 2 1 2 1   R P (1 sixth 5) 4 3 2 3 2 3 2

Bill Grogan's Goat
Duet for Playing and Singing

Southern Appalachian Folksong
Arr. R C Hayden

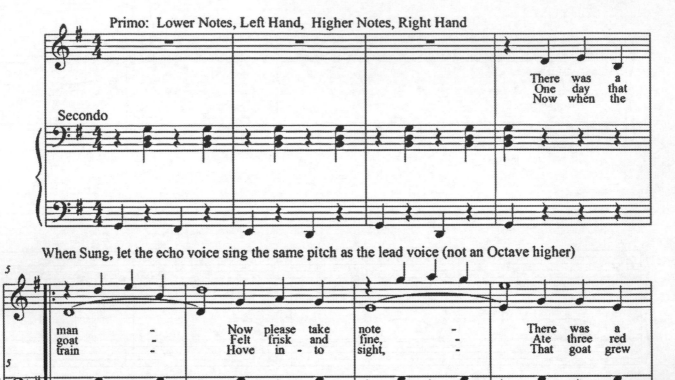

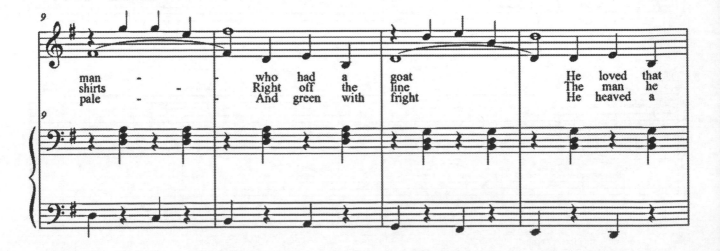

Bill Grogan's Goat

The Hayden Family, Roger is the little guy in the front, about 13, already playing piano
For five years. We loved singing "Bill Grogan's Goat"

Hand Over Hand Arpeggios

Rank and File

The Soldiers march all straight and true
In Rank and File beneath the blue
The Flag in front, their feet in step
And trained to keep our Freedom new.

Things you can do with chords

R C Hayden

FP 5 4 5 3 4 2 3 1   H P (5) 3 4 2 3 1 2 1   RP (1) 5 4 5 2 4 2 3

Autumn Winds and Autumn Leaves

Stems up, Right hand
Stems Down, Left hand

for
Krista Hayden who lives in Bangkok
by Grampa R C Hayden

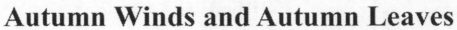

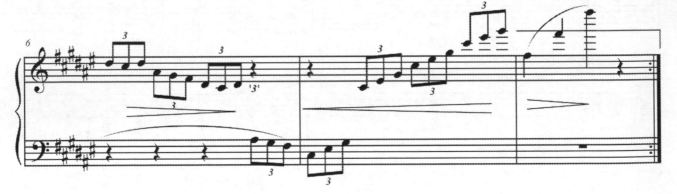

Autumn Winds and Autumn Leaves

How Firm A Foundation

Traditional Hymn

2. "Fear not, I am with you, O be not dismayed; for I am your God, and will still give you aid;
I'll strengthen you, help you, and cause you to stand, upheld by my righteous, omnipotent hand.

3. "When through the deep waters I call you to go, the rivers of sorrow shall not overflow;
For I will be with you, your troubles to bless, and sanctify to you your deepest distress.

6. "The soul that on Jesus has leaned for repose, I will not, I will not desert to his foes;
That soul, though all hell should endeavor to shake, I'll never, no never, no never forsake.

Ripon's Selection of Hymns: 1787

F P 1 2 3 4 3 4 3 5 4   H P (5) 4 2 3 (1) 2 3 4   RP (1) sixth 5 3 4 2 3

Cool Dark Cave

The air is cool, chill and damp
Still and silent, dark and dank
Stone hard, stone cold air
A little fear while breathing here
Shiver and brrrrr.

R C Hayden

Spring Sunrise

Demonstrate/Imitate

Early Black Key Song
Don't forget the C flats !

R C Hayden

With cautious pedaling, listening, and lifting pedal when dissonance becomes offending.

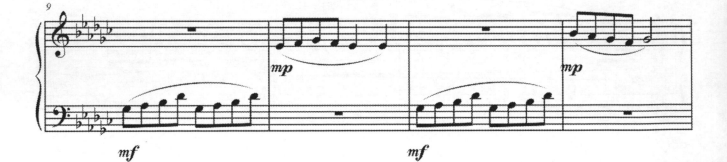

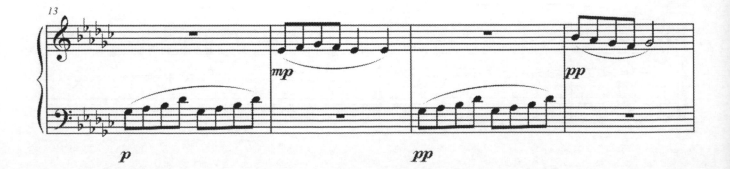

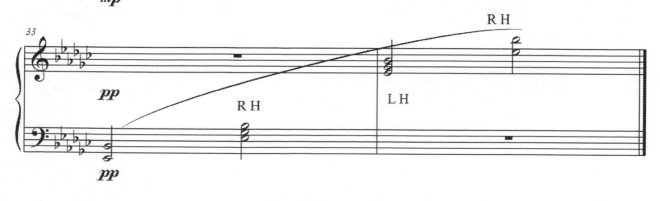

F P 5 3 4 2 3 1   H P (3) 4 2 5 1 5 1 5   R P (5) 1 4 2 3 2 3 1

Chipmunk

for Krista

R C Hayden

Fairmount Park
Revisited

Triplet Rhythm Scales are great coordination and rhythm trainers and a little more fun to do.

R C Hayden

Fairmount Park

Triplet Rhythm One Octave Scale

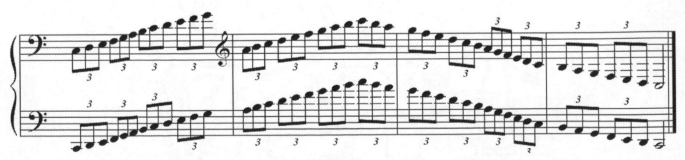

Triplet Rhythm Three Octave Scale

Triplet Scales in D, E, G and A

Old Art Pratt

Zipp, zupp, zipp, zupp, cuttin' up the firewood
One stick, two stick, 'nuff for all the winter
Saw it up, stack it up, gotta keep the house warm
Cook the food, boil the pot, can't stop, need a lot.

R C Hayden

F P 1 5 2 5 3 5   H P (5) 4 1 4 2 4 1 4   R P (1 seventh 5) 2 3 2

A morning hike into the vale
The mists obscurring tree and hill
Damp and cool, chill and green,
Footsteps soft, the sun unseen
A pleasant place to think and dream.

Misty Vale

R C Hayden

Write in your own Tempo and Expressions

Note the title and poem.   Play the notes and listen. Write on the blank below a tempo
marking that fits. Then add appropriate dynamic markings for each hand.

A couple of ritardandos (rit.) are suggested by the music, both will need 'a tempo" to
bring the music back to the original tempo.

R C Hayden

Ripples

There once was a little motif
That kept coming back in repeat
And we spotted the trick, our eyes caught it real quick
And we read and we played instantly!!

R C Hayden

Brethren, We Have Met to Worship

Music: William Moore, 19th century
arr. R C Hayden

Words: George Atkins

Contemplation

R C Hayden

To sit and think and look inside at what I want to be and do;
One cannot find these secret thoughts unless you stop and think it through.
A life is not made up of games or empty talk or running fast,
It's looking for the things to do that live in hearts with joy that lasts.

F P 4 3 2 5 4 3 2 1   H P 1 4 3 (2) 5 4 5 4   R P 1 octave (5) 4 3 2 3 2 3

Night Rider

R C Hayden

Sonatina in G
The Shifting Hands

Spirito

R C Hayden

R C Hayden

The Secret Path

R C Hayden

The Bear Song

Bears are hungry, strong and furry
If they're close you ought to worry
Walk away,and do not hurry
Bears are hungry, strong and furry

Demonstrate/Imitate

R C Hayden

With a pencil, add dynamic signs and articulations where it seems the music is leading. There are lots of possibilities and interesting variations to bring the music alive expressively.

Dew Dance

In the early morning when the dew is in the air
First sun through the leaves, the mists rise everywhere.
Dancing in the rising rays with colors, hues and sheens,
Twisting, turning, glowing golden, white with light and green.

R C Hayden

All the accidentals make this look hard. But it is NOT. See patterns, see intervals, 'break the code', it's easy!

Walking the Tightrope
Get me to the Other Side

R C Hayden

F P 3 4 3 2 1 2 3 1   H P (4) 3 1 2 1 2   R P (1-5) 3 3 2 2 4 4 3

The Runner

R C Hayden

Presto

accel.

How Sweet and Awesome Is the Place

Reverently

Old Irish Hymn Melody

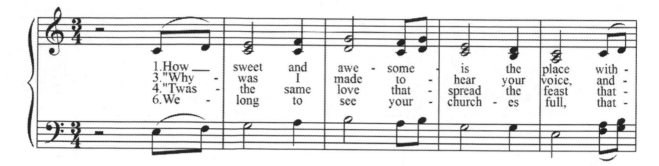

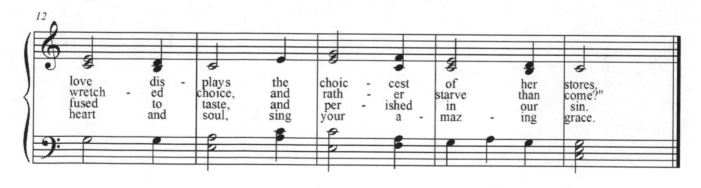

F P 2 4 5 4 3 4 3 4   H P (1) 3 4 3 5 4 3 2   R P (1-5) 4 3 4 3 2 4 3

Arabesque

Allegro Scherzando

Friedrich Burgmuller

Minuet

from the Songbook of
Anna Magdalena Bach

You can discern fingering by observing where phrases begin and the range they cover. Write in just enough finger numbers to guide the changing hand positions and play it musically and intelligently.

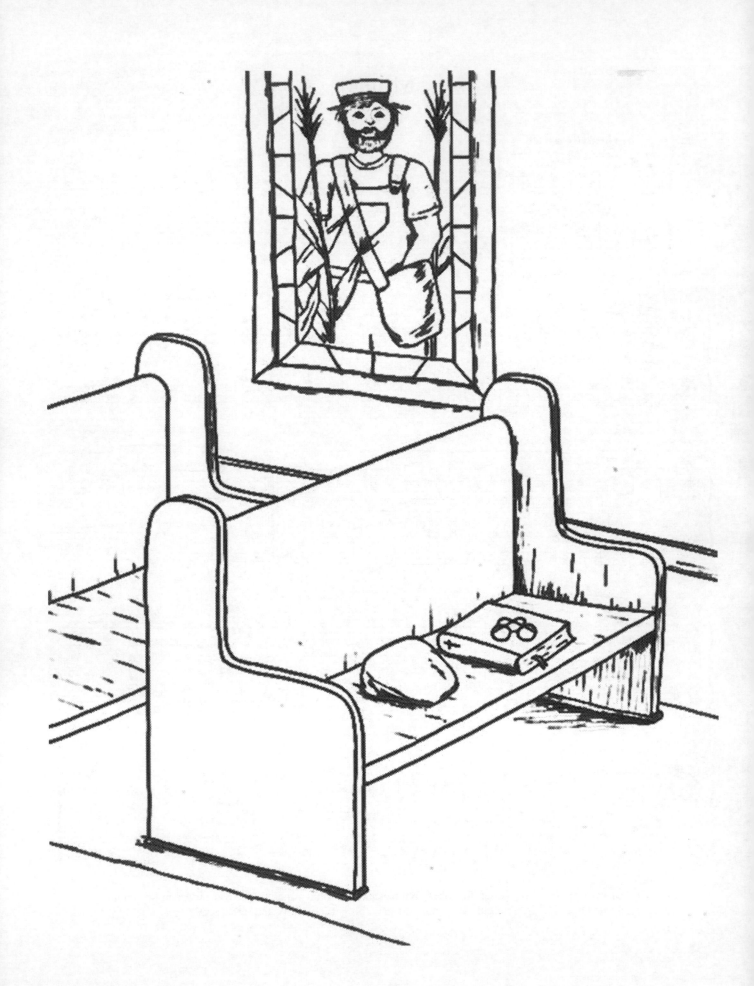

How Sweet and Awesome Is the Place

For Niall O'Neill

Piano Solo

Old Irish Hymn Melody

Following are suggested collections that are within reach of your acquired reading and technic.

There is no end to other valuable lessons to be learned. The HAPI Book is designed to equip you to read and play more interesting piano literature quickly. As you reach for the music that you love most you can expect this foundation to serve you.

Easy Classics to Moderns Vol 17 Denes Agay	ISBN 9780825640179
Essential Classics, Vol. I: Bach to Gurlitt	ISBN 000308097252
Essential Classics, Vol. II: Handel to Tchaikovsky	ISBN 000308097269
Essential Keyboard Duets Vol 1 Janet Vogt	ISBN 0739020293
Jazz, Rags and Blues, Volumes 1 (of 5) by Martha Mier Vol 1	ISBN 038081020488
Romantic Impressions Book 1 by Martha Mier	ISBN 9780739006177
Preludes Vandall 24 Original Piano Solos in All Major and Minor Keys	ISBN 9780739043172
Bagatelles Vol 1 R Vandall	ISBN 038081242415
Piano Treasury of Easy Classical Music	ISBN 9780825634833 Amsco Pub.
Hanon The Virtuoso Pianist in Sixty Exercises	ISBN 9780793525447

There are many more fine collections, composers and arrangers. Seek out music at the Early Intermediate Level. Stay aware of the widest interval your hand can reach comfortably, do not choose music that stays at that interval without rest.

Websites that can help:

www.sheetmusicplus.com

www.alfred-music.com

www.musicnotes.com

www.amazon.com search for piano sheet music

Weekly Finger Patterns Sequence

Originator
Anne Vanko Liva
Compiled & Arr. R C Hayden

Assign one pattern (measure) each week. Each measure is performed beginning on middle C, repeated on D, E,F etc. to the C above. Left hand begins on C and moves down one key at a time.

Weekly Hold Pattern Sequence

Originator
Anne Vanko Liva

R C Hayden

Assign one pattern (measure) each week. The Left Hand performs the same pattern beginning
on Middle C and moving down the keys.
Each Right Hand pattern is done once starting on C, then moves up to D, E, F, etc. for one octave.
Left Hand begings on middle C, and moves down to B, A, G, etc. for one octave.
Always perform them rhythmically, with energy and evenness of touch, listening constantly.

Weekly Reach Patterns Sequence

Assign one pattern (measure) each week. The Left Hand performs the same pattern beginning
on Middle C and moving down the keys.
Each Right Hand pattern is done once starting on C, then moves up to D, E, F, etc. for one octave.
Left Hand begings on middle C, and moves down to B, A, G, etc. for one octave.
Always perform them rhythmically, with energy and evenness of touch, listening constantly.

Other Useful Keyboard Lessons
Musical Calisthetics that Teach and Equip

Compiled by
R C Hayden

The HAPI Book, its methods and pieces have been tested and found profitable in many studios since 2011. It has been used in Pennsylvania, New York, Texas, Connecticut, Massachusetts, California, Washington and even Bangkok.

You will PLAY NOW, and learn as you go. It is a multi-skilled, multi-gifted approach that fits many learning styles; whether you learn by ear, eye, touch, or mostly intellect, the HAPI Book gets everybody playing and READING!

Ages seven and beyond excel quickly. Come with a childlike heart and let your fingers fly.

A HAPI Primary edition for ages four to six is planned for the Summer of 2015. CAUTION: NOT ALL small children are ready for piano lessons, do not risk failure by starting too soon. Giftedness is not always evident in the very young. The Primary HAPI Book will be meant to bring accessible delights to very little learners.

Please note: Parenting is the most important element in creating young musicians. Unlike most sports, the magic of practice takes place at home. Parents MUST BE READY to be cheerfully and patiently involved and to enable the child to be faithful and intense with their practice. Make time in each day, sit with the little ones, visit and encourage every age. You need not know anything about music, you do need to love and nurture all that is good, forgive the mistakes, and put joy into their performing for you. Let them teach you a thing or two, (teachers are always learning from students). Do not expect them to always love practicing, nor to always find their own incentive. Good parenting carries them through the low times. And when honest work brings real progress, only poor parenting lets them quit.

For the more mature beginner, **faithfulness** will become your vehicle of achievement. **Go** to the piano even when you don't feel like it. **Find time**. Always perform the **finger patterns** (you don't need a piano to do them). Assume you are growing (even when it doesn't 'feel' like it). **Get help** when you are stuck, it's probably a simple solution. Stubborn independence can leave you climbing walls when all you need is a key to the door; get help.

Avoid *Perfectionism*, it is unrealistic and limiting. Avoid the curse of *Pride*. Music is for the joy of it, don't hide while you strive, nor let accomplishment become a badge of honor. Instead, let it be a blessing to all around you. Neither give nor receive painful criticism. Be an encourager. And be encouraged. You can do this!

Go to: www.haydenpiano.com for additional helps and videos.

Printed in the United States
By Bookmasters